HEALTHY FOODS

Diet Secrets for Wealthy Nutrition

Joe Brown

© 2020

INTRODUCTION

Are you conflicted about all the nutritional advice out there?

Are you exhausted with all those strict diet limitations that require you to be unrealistically thin?

Do you feel like all these diets just end up making you feel guilty about eating all those foods you love?

Well, this e-book discussion centers around the 15 foods that studies and sources have researched and looked into exhaustively across Western Europe and the United States and have been deemed as the most healthful. This e-book using simple tips can help you cut across all the confusion and stick to a nutrient-filled diet that is beneficial to your body as well as your mind.

Some diets on the extremes may teach otherwise but we do require an equilibrium of all the major nutrients in our diet for a healthy body. There is no need to rule out certain foods, rather wise selections of the healthiest alternatives from every category is the best approach.

You see, healthy eating is about improving your overall health, your productivity and enhancing your mental and emotional composure. Healthy foods options must not always be difficult or complicated. However, it is overwhelming, all these conflicting theories, where today an expert says a you should only consume some certain food types for better health certain and tomorrow another expert tells you the exact opposite.

Truth is that while some foods providing certain nutrients are known to be beneficial on your overall mood, the baseline is your complete diet outline that is of most importance. Most importantly replacing processed foods with healthier alternatives should be the first priority. Consuming foods that are as close as possible to their natural form can make a significant difference to your overall health.

In this e-book, after deep, well thought and well-researched information, all these healthy options will be broken down one after another so that you will be able to understand your choices. After reading this book you will be able to actively start on the process of making healthy choices to achieve a fulfilling life.

This is not just about freedom from illness, it is a commitment to change, progress and growth. This is because a healthy lifestyle will affect our every emotion either positively or negatively. In the end, our thoughts and actions are directly affected. It is like an endless circle. It is, therefore, crucial for everyone to work towards achieving a healthy diet to reduce illness, reduce stress and improve on positive interactions.

Contents

CHAPTER ONE

The Healthiest Foods

When shopping, this should be a basic rule; Simple, wholesome, plant-based foods and spices are the best options. Avoid pre-packaged foods that have a long list of unfamiliar ingredients. Using the nutrient density concept (That is, a measure of how much nutrient a type of food contains in comparison to its calories) we have come up with a list of foods that will give you all the important nutrients for excellent health.

Fruits and Vegetables
Naturally, fruits and vegetables should be included in every healthy meal. That is because they contain minerals and vitamins that help boost overall health. Each day it is recommended that you eat at least two servings of fruit and five servings of vegetables as a part of a balanced diet and active lifestyle. There are different colors and varieties to choose from and they come in many ways of cooking, preparation, and serving.

American Heart Association

Fruits

They are the fleshy, sweet parts of plants that can be eaten. Generally, they have seeds. They can be eaten raw or cooked depending on the variety.

The common types are

- Berries e.g. blueberries, strawberries, raspberries, passionfruit
- Melons e.g. honeydew melons, watermelons, rockmelons
- Exotic and tropical e.g. mangoes, bananas
- Stone variety e.g. plums, peaches, nectarines
- Citrus fruits e.g. lemon, lime, grapefruits, citron, oranges
- Tomatoes and avocados
- Apples and pears

Zucchini Greengrocers LTD

Vegetables

When classified into biological groups they include

- Root vegetables e.g. sweet potatoes, yams, Irish potatoes
- Leafy greens e.g. spinach kales, lettuce, silverbeet

- Allium e.g. shallot, onions, garlic
- Cruciferous e.eg. broccoli, cabbage, Brussels, broccoli, sprouts
- Marrow e.g. pumpkins, zucchini, cucumber

- Edible plant stem e.g. asparagus, celery. Goodhousekeeping.com

Nutritional Comparisons Between Fruits and Vegetables

These two are quite similar in terms of levels of nutrition. They are both high in not only vitamins but also fibers. In addition to that, they are also high in plant compounds, minerals, and anti-oxidants.

Naturally, they both contain low levels of fats and sodium. However, as you might already know given their sweet nature, fruits contain more natural sugars as well as calories compared to vegetables.

Furthermore, for the same weight, leafy vegetables contain less fiber compared to certain fruits. For example, per every 100 grams of fruit, the fiber content would be around 3-14 grams while vegetables contain 1-4 grams of fiber per 100 grams.

However, leafy vegetables contain higher water content, from 84-95% water, while most fruits contain less water, which is around 61-89% water.

The nutritional differences vary amongst different vegetables and fruits as well, for instance, tubers are vegetables but they are very rich in fiber as well as vitamins C and B and potassium.

Vegetable and fruit Colors

Vegetables and fruits with similar colors have the same valuable compounds. For example

- Greens: Vegetables such as spinach contain vitamins like lutein that are important for vitamin A.
- White vegetables; an example is a cauliflower which contains sulforaphane
- Red food; Watermelons, beetroots, and tomatoes contain lycopene.
- Blue or purple vegetables; like the eggplant and blueberries contain anthocyanins.

To get maximum nutrients, serve multiple types of vegetables and fruits. It is also important to buy those foods that are in season so that you get maximum quality. You can also get creative while serving vegetables and fruits. For example, make vegetable soup, vegetable salads, stir-fried meats and vegetables, dried or canned fruits, and raw vegetables as well.

123RF.Com

Preparations for Fruits and Vegetables

Over-processing of foods damages nutrients and phytochemicals in plant-based foods. The same applies to vegetables even though they are usually cooked. Here are a few suggestions on how you can maximize your fruits and vegetables;

- Blend them into your smoothies
- Try eating them raw as much as you can
- Grill, microwave, bake, steam or stir-fry using unsaturated oils on nonstick pans
- Never overcook your vegetables
- Serve them alongside sauces, salsas and vegetable pesto's
- Always cut your vegetables and fruits using sharp knives to avoid bruises

Once prepared, take the time to make the food visually appealing. A tasty meal that is full of variety will be more likely enjoyed than plain meals.

Meat, Eggs, Fish and Chicken

For the body to grow and develop, the foods in this group must be eaten for their proteins. These foods provide the protein needed for tissue growth and repair. They also contain vitamin B, magnesium, zinc and iron which is needed for the formation of healthy blood.

Meat

Generally speaking, the nutritional value of a particular kind of meat varies widely not just with the kind of meat but also with its quality.

- Pork is a rich source of thiamin
- Liver stores and is therefore rich in folic acid, vitamin A and riboflavin.
- Meat is an excellent source of minerals such as zinc, magnesium, and potassium in addition to vitamin B-6 and B-12.
- In many cultures also, the internal organs of animals are considered delicacies

21bites

Fish

Fish species such as the cod store fats in the liver. As a result, they are packed with vitamins and oils in their lean muscles.

Oily Fish

Fish oil, unlike the fat from land animals, is rich in fatty acids. Some examples of fish such as salmon, herring and trout store oils and tissues around their gut and tissues. Their fillets contain omega 3 acids.

ANAD

Eggs

Eggs are versatile and can, therefore, be easily incorporated into balanced meals. Egg yolk contains most of the vitamins and is rich in vitamins A, B-2, B-12 and proteins. Its white also contains proteins and essential amino acids. Eggs are also rich in irons and calcium. The vitamins in eggs are important in the generation of healthy red blood cells and the preservation of energy.

Natasha'skitchen.com

Chicken

Chicken is a healthy source of protein, however, that depends on the mode of preparation for the meal. You should minimize the consumption of deep-fried chicken. Chicken skin is also high in saturated fats which you most likely want to avoid.

Inspiredkitchen.net

Grains, Seeds and Nuts

Grains

They are packed with complex carbohydrates and fiber and are at the base of most food pyramids. Whole grains are the best choice because they contain bran that allows for key nutrients such as vitamin E to be retained by the body. Other healthy grains include brown rice, barley, and quinoa.

Seeds

Ground seeds are high in protein, fats, and fiber. Some good options are

- Flax,
- chia,
- sunflower,
- hemp
- sesame

Nuts

Fats from nuts protect from heart disease and joint degeneration. They release energy slowly so that you feel fuller for longer. Hazelnuts, for instance, are high in antioxidants. Nuts also speed up recovery from exercise and muscle repair.

When shopping for grains buy those which are unprocessed, whole varieties.

Milk and Milk Products

Milk and dairy products are important in children's diets. They contain calcium for the development of strong bones and teeth in infants.

NewFood Magazine.com

CHAPTER TWO:

Superfoods

Superfood is a term that has been recently used to refer to those foods that provide you with a higher nutrient density in comparison to their calories. They are mostly plant-based but can also include fish and dairy. Superfoods are thought to have the capacity to positively improve health. That's because they contain high amounts of vitamins, minerals, nutrients, and antioxidants for smaller amounts of calories.

People have unrealistic expectations of these foods, thinking they can prevent them from getting chronic health issues. They eat a few of them on an overall poor diet. Superfoods should be included as part of a daily healthy diet intake. Try a super diet rather than having a one food mindset. Eating vegetables and fruits regularly has been associated with lower lifestyle-related health complications

The term superfood is fairly new, having been invented by marketers to promote sales. This term has no legal definitions or standard formula that applies to the foods at this time. It does not also refer to a specific food group. According to the American Heart Association, there is not a spelled-out criterion for those foods that are considered superfoods and those that are not. Most of them are however plant-based.

Here we will try and discuss the foods that are considered as superfoods giving examples as well as tips on how you can include them in your diet.

Dark Green Leafy Vegetables

These vegetables are packed with nutrients. They are a good source of calcium, zinc, iron, magnesium vitamin C and fiber. Leafy vegetables contain anti-inflammatory compounds also known as carotenoids that can protect against cancer. Leafy greens also have a high-water content that prevents constipation and improves overall digestion

Examples include;

- Spinach
- Kales
- Swiss chard
- Collards
- Turnips

Get creative with the dark green leafy vegetables that have a bitter taste. You can include them in smoothies, soups, and salads.

shutterstock.com • 390988804

Legumes (including Soy)

Legumes are inclusive of peas, lentils, peanuts, and beans. They have a huge variation in appearance, nutritional value, use, and taste as well. Legumes therefore generally refer to the seeds of the leguminous plants. In many cultures around the world, they are a staple food because they are not just cheap, but they are also amongst the best sources of plant-based proteins.

They are superfoods because they are rich in minerals, proteins, fiber, and vitamin B. Because they release energy gradually, they help you feel satisfied much longer. They, therefore, help in the maintenance of a healthy weight. Research shows that they have numerous health benefits such as reduced cholesterol levels and the management of type two diabetes.

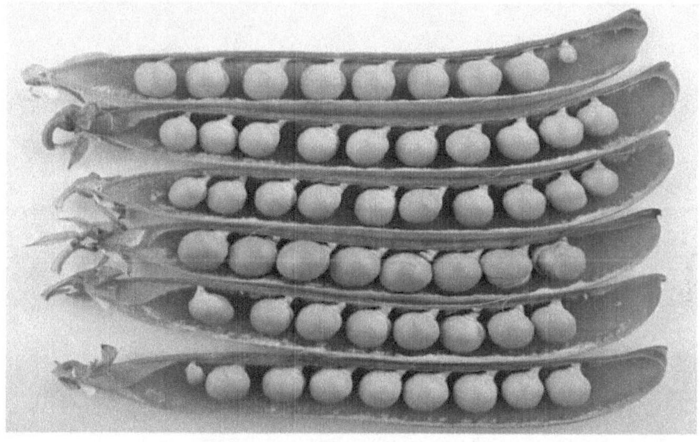

Hosokawa Micron Powder

Berries

Berries are considered a nutritional powerhouse because they contain exceptional levels of antioxidants, minerals, and fiber. The good thing is they can be multifunctional, they are excellent as part of your breakfast, can be eaten as a dessert or on salads and smoothies.

The most common berries include

- Blackberries
- Goji berries
- Acai berries
- Strawberries
- Blueberries
- Cranberries
- Raspberries
- Tart cherries

Goji berries are native to Asia and are used frequently in Eastern medicine. Acai berries are native to South America and they contain up to 19 amino acids. Acai berry powder is also available to purchase online.

Green Tea

Originally from China, green tea is rich in Catechins that have anti-inflammatory and anti-carcinogenic benefits. Green tea is known to suppress inflammation and can, therefore have anti-arthritic benefits. A study published by the *Journal of Physiological Anthropology* examining the effects of white tea, green tea and water consumption on 18 students on stress levels suggested that green tea and white tea had reduced levels of stress on the individuals.

One of the main antioxidants in tea called epigallocatechin gallate gives green its ability to protect from diseases. Research has also shown that caffeine in combination with catechins in tea makes it an important tool for weight loss.

IsItUnhealthy.com

Olive oil

Olive oil is extracted naturally from the fruits of the olive tree. It is a main part of the Mediterranean diet. Due to its monounsaturated fatty acids, olive oil is considered to be very healthy. It contains antioxidants that reduce inflammation and protect against oxidative stress and cell damage. In the long run, olive oil is quite instrumental in reducing the risks of diabetes, heart diseases, and inflammation.

There is also evidence of changes linked to longevity when you exercise after consuming olive oil. Not only is olive oil beneficial when consumed, but it is also often applied to the skin and hair. Olive oil strengthens the hair and keeps it healthy and can also be used as a treatment before shampooing the hair. No wonder olive oil is popularly known as "liquid gold"

It comes in a few varieties

- Extra Virgin Olive Oil; It is costly and not everyone can afford it. It is made by cold pressing the olive fruit. It is considered the best variety for our bodies.
- Virgin Olive Oil; is the best known and most popular variety of olive oil. It has a low acid content and is recommended for people who want to enjoy the benefits of olive oil without breaking their banks for it.
- Lamp ante Oil; Not suitable for cooking. It is only used as a fuel
- Pure Olive Oil; Has high acid content and is not recommended for cooking. It is a combination of the virgin and the extra virgin olive oils.

Ginger and Garlic

Garlic is used as a culinary ingredient because of its flavor. It is closely related to onions and shallots. For centuries, garlic has been used in medicine due to its benefits. Garlic is a good source of fiber, vitamin B-6, C, manganese, and selenium. Furthermore, garlic may play a role in reducing the risk of cancer. Research has also proven that garlic supports the immune functions of the body and helps reduce cholesterol in the long run

Ginger, on the other hand, is a root product of a plant originally from China. It is used to enhance the flavor of food in addition to its health benefits. The roots of the ginger plant contain gingerol which is an antioxidant with numerous medicinal effects. Ginger treats nausea, colds, flu and prevents chronic illnesses. It also effectively manages pain from chronic and acute inflammation.

Mushrooms

The most common varieties include oyster mushrooms, button, cremini, and portobello. The nutritional value depends on the type of mushroom but generally, they contain fiber, antioxidants, potassium and vitamin A. They range from the more common puffballs that are an everyday fare to the more costly truffles that are considered a delicacy.

According to the Agricultural Marketing Resource Centre, in 2015, each person in the United States consumed around 3 pounds of mushrooms. Mushrooms are thought to be associated with more vegetable consumption. In the end, they contribute to an overall nutritious diet. Another advantage worth noting with mushrooms is that it is grown from agricultural waste products. This means that they are environmentally friendly and they are also sustainable.

Nature.com

CHAPTER 3

The Top Health Benefits of Eating Healthy

Eating healthy means eating different types of fruits, whole grains, vegetables, lean proteins, healthy fats, and starch. While eating healthy, always avoid foods rich in salt and sugar. Here are some of the top benefits of eating healthy.

Bakingbusiness.com

Improved Heart Health

Medical conditions that principally involve blood vessels and the heart has risen in recent years. A study conducted in the US in 2017 found that more than 92.1 million people in the US suffer at least one type of cardiovascular disease. On the other hand, in Canada, Heart and stroke foundation found that 80% of these diseases can be prevented by a change of lifestyle. The best way to change your lifestyle is by engaging in more physical activities and above all eating healthy.

Studies have also found that foods rich in vitamin E help in preventing blood clots. As we know blood clots cause heart attacks. Foods such as almonds, sunflower seeds, peanuts, green vegetables, and hazelnuts are best at providing the body with vitamin E. Moreover, medics have long identified a strong relationship between coronary heart diseases and trans unsaturated fatty acids. Therefore, if you eliminate trans fats from your diet, you at least reduce the risk of contracting such heart-related illnesses.

A reduction in trans fats reduces the level of low-density lipoprotein cholesterol which would have otherwise caused plaque to collect in the arteries. An increased deposit of plaque results in an increased risk of stroke and other related diseases. Also, reducing the level of salt intake to 1,500 mg per day helps with reducing blood pressure hence better heart health.

Eating Healthy Helps with Weight Loss
Having a high weight or being obese increases the risk of contracting chronic diseases such as; cancer, diabetes mellitus, heart diseases, and poor bone density. However, losing weight can help reduce the risk or contain such diseases. If you are looking to lose weight, take whole vegetables and fruits that are low in calories.

Avoid processed foods as most of them are higher in calories. Besides, you can determine your daily calorie intake by using dietary guidelines that are available online. For instance, add more fiber to your diet. A lot of dietary fiber is found in most plants. The best thing with fiber is that it makes you feel fuller for longer periods.

A study conducted in 2018 found that with fiber and lean proteins, you can reduce weight without having to count your daily calorie intake.

Geminiresearchnews.com

Reduced Risk of Cancer
American Society of Oncology reported in 2014 that obesity leads to a worse outlook for patients suffering from cancer. Keeping an unhealthful diet leads to obesity which in turn leads to an increase in a person's risk of cancer. This is why you should aim to weigh within a healthy range to reduce the risk.

Another study in 2014 also found that eating fruits reduced the risk of cancer in the upper gastrointestinal tract. Similarly, they found that eating fibers and fruits reduced the risk of colorectal cancer while eating lots of fibers reduced the risk of contracting liver cancer. Fruits, vegetables, and legumes have phytochemicals that act as antioxidants. The antioxidants (vitamins E, C, and A, beta-carotene, and lycopene) are known to protect cells from damage which leads to cancer.

A Healthy Gut

The human colon has natural bacteria in it that play important roles in metabolism. Certain types of bacteria produce vitamins B and K for the benefit of the colon. A diet that is high in sugars and less in fibers leads to inflammation in the colon. However, a diet that is rich in vegetables, grains and whole legumes produce both prebiotics and probiotics that aid the bacteria to thrive.

In addition, take fermented foods such as kimchi, yogurt, and miso that are rich in probiotics. Regular intake of fiber also aids in regular bowel movements reducing the risk of bowel cancer and diverticulitis.

Foods you Need to Cut off From Your Diet

With all the healthy options available, moderation is the most important thing. As much as dark chocolate is beneficial to your health, too many sweets will make you gain weight. A little wine is good for your heart, but we have all seen the worst side of alcoholism. Some foods, however, have zero beneficial qualities to your health. These foods should be avoided at all costs.

Refined Sugars

In fruits, sugar occurs naturally. These natural sugars are not harmful at all.

Healthydesigns.net

Added sugars, however, in sweets, coffees, tea, and juice increase the risks of heart disease while adding no nutritional value to your body. Furthermore, once you make refined sugar an occasional indulgence your body craves them when you have not consumed them. Start by cutting off one bad habit at a time and replace it with other healthier alternatives.

"Fat-Free" Foods

The term has been recently used as a psychological tool by marketers for the wrong regular versions of foods. Most likely, people who have this idea of fat-free foods overeat them thinking it's okay. These foods also make you feel less guilty by shifting the blame. The processed fat-free foods people love also replace fat with a lot of sugars. For that reason, they are no good for a healthy diet. Natural fat-free foods like fruits and vegetables are good for your health.

Webmd.com

Soda

They are a tasty combination of caffeine and sugar and they make for a good quick fix. But it doesn't matter if they come in the regular, diet or zero sugar variety there is no value addition to your healthy diet choice. Soda lovers will most of the time weigh more than people who do not take sodas regularly. Eventually, soda is a predisposing factor to type 2 diabetes among other lifestyle diseases.

Exporters India

White Bread, Rice and Pasta

White bread is outright bad. It has a low nutritional value and makes it easier to gain weight. The same applies to pasta and white rice. Once digested, they turn into sugars that cause tooth decay. There are healthier substitutes such as brown whole grain rice and bread. The whole grain alternatives have a higher fiber content that is healthy for you.

Dreamstime.com

Refined Meat

Homemade grilled chicken and beef are cheaper and healthier. There is absolutely no reason why you should consume the sodium packed processed meats that predispose you to colon cancer and high blood pressure.

Cancer Treatment Centre.

CHAPTER 4

Processed foods are Bad!! Why you Should Stop Consuming Processed Foods!

Whether it was cereal in the morning, beef at lunch or dinner, chances are that today you have taken some processed foods. A part of your diet most likely contains some of the refined, preserved or messed-around Package that lies on our stores' shelves.

Processed foods are the number one contributor to illnesses and obesity around the world. The question is how do we know? It is not news that when people follow the western diet that mainly consists of processed foods, they become sick. Adopting these foods for just a few years has huge effects on such people. It is obvious that their genetic makeup did not change, what changed is the food intake.

There exists a lot of arguments and confusion about the word "processed". This is what I mean. Of course, majority of foods that we eat are processed in a way. For instance, beef can be minced and apples picked from trees, still this is processing. However, the difference is that some foods are mechanically processed while others are chemically processed. The latter is the main offender.

Generally, the best definition of processed foods is those that are processed chemically and have artificial ingredients added to them.

Bing.com

Reasons Why you Should Avoid Processed Foods
High levels of sugar
With processed foods, be sure to consume lots of sugar accompanied by high fructose corn syrup. It is very extensive, for instance, a study found that 90% of added sugar comes from processed foods and beverages. As we all know, excess sugar is very harmful. Although sugar provides energy, it has empty calories and is not nutritious.

Several pieces of research have shown that sugar has adverse effects on metabolism making the "empty" calorie to be just the tip of the iceberg. High sugar levels lead to; abdominal cavity, increased accumulation of fats in the liver, insulin resistance, increased cholesterol, and increased triglycerides.

As a result, the world worse killers such as obesity, cancer, diabetes, and heart diseases are all associated with sugar consumption. Even though most people avoid putting sugar in their cereals and coffee, most sugars are derived from processed foods and beverages.

Processed Foods are Addictive

You can't just eat one piece? Certainly, there is a scientific explanation behind your all-time favorite snack. Several processed foods are chemically altered to release dopamine, a neurotransmitter that is reward-related when eaten. For this reason, many people struggle with food addiction, especially processed foods.

Food addiction is a problem for modern society although most people don't acknowledge it.
Recent studies have also shown that junk foods and sugars activate the areas in the brain as drugs such as cocaine.

Less Fiber

Fiber, both fermentable and soluble fibers have many benefits. Soluble fiber aids in reducing constipation. Fiber gives the ability to feel full with fewer calories as it slows down the absorption of carbohydrates. Most processed foods don't have fiber as it is intentionally removed during the processing.

Reduced Nutrients

Whole unprocessed foods have more nutrients than chemically processed foods. Although sometimes during the processing, synthetic vitamins are added to those foods, they cannot be compared to the nutrients found in whole food. No doubt, whole foods contain more than just vitamins and minerals. Plants and animals have a variety of nutrients that are still being discovered today.

Perhaps someday human beings will invent a chemical blend of all the nutrients, but before that; just eat whole healthy foods.

Leads to Overconsumption
It is human nature to want food. Appetites lean towards food that is sweet, fatty and salty to taste. Food manufacturers will, therefore, strive to come up with the best foods. With increased competition, each manufacturer produces foods that are the most rewarding and desirable.

According to evolutionary history, human beings have a body and brain mechanism that regulates energy balance. It worked so well until recently to keep people healthy. However, in recent studies, the momentary value of food can exceed this normal mechanism. As a result, you end up eating more food. The overconsumption of food then compromises your health.

Processed foods are so rewarding that they affect our behavior and thoughts. We then eat too much until we become ill.

Increased Refined Carbohydrates
Some people think that energy should be derived from cabs while some prefer to avoid carbohydrates like plague. Regardless of these two opinions, we can agree that carbohydrates from unprocessed foods are the best.

Processed foods have refined carbohydrates that are easily broken leading to increased blood sugar and insulin amount. A few hours later, blood sugar reduces, you again start craving for carbohydrates. This process is known as the " blood sugar roller coaster". No wonder the ingestion of refined carbs leads to chronic diseases. If you eat processed foods just before bedtime, it can sabotage your sleep. Your body struggles to deal with the high strikes of insulin and sugar, you may just find yourself tossing and turning.

Contains Several Artificial Ingredients
Try to read the ingredients on some of these artificial foods. Chances are you may not understand most of them. Most of these ingredients are artificial chemicals. The processed food normally contains; texture chemicals, colorants, preservatives and flavor. Additionally, some manufacturers might add chemicals and not disclose them.
Although the chemicals have been tested to be safe, artificial ingredients aren't the healthiest.

High Levels of Trans Fat
Processed foods have refined vegetable oils and seeds that are hydrogenated turning them into trans fats. Vegetable oil intake among people is so high which is unhealthy. Vegetable oils contains high amounts of fatty acids that causes inflammation. A recent study confirmed that people consume a lot of vegetable oil leading to an increased rate of heart diseases. Also, the main cause of death in western countries is heart diseases. If it is hydrogenated fats it even becomes worse. Trans fats are at far the worst substance you can ingest to your body. Instead, use olive oil or coconut oil.

Less Time for Digestion
Processed foods can easily melt in your mouth. They are easier to chew and swallow. Most ingredients are refined and fiber taken out therefore you can digest it faster and eat more. As a result, when you take processed foods you burn fewer calories per day by half compared to when you take whole foods.

CHAPTER 5

Ending Food Confusion and Misconceptions

There exist several factors that make healthy eating complicated and confusing. For a long time, the topic of nutrition has attracted lots of research and different views on it. It should not be so overwhelming as food is fundamental to human beings. Besides, food is natural to us. We all know that food functions to energize, heal and repair our bodies.

Anything you ingest has a powerful opportunity to either heal or harm your body. Ask yourself what type of food you want in your body. Is it the real food that comes from the earth or processed foods that makes you sick? There are numerous misconceptions about food.

Misconceptions on Healthy Eating

For several years people have been confused and carry the misconceptions along with them. As a result, the misconceptions are passed from one generation to another. Unfortunately, these misconceptions about healthy eating contribute to the growing cases of chronic diseases and obesity amongst us. Luckily, recent research findings provide the truth about the misconceptions backed with meaningful scientific explanations.

You should Never Cheat on a Diet
A common myth about food, nutrition, and diet is the misconception that you should never " cheat" on a diet.
Sometimes it is alright to overeat a little. A registered dietitian and nutritionist in the UK, Nichola Whitehead suggests that is perfectly fine to go off a strict diet once in a while. Overeating regularly is the bad habit that leads to weight gain, she added. Also, switching from a diet full of processed carbohydrates and red meat to taking vegetables, lean proteins and grains is a good step towards a positive direction.

Jump Start your Diet by Cleansing and Detoxing
The human body has a natural detoxing system. So, unless you have been poised there is no need for a detox. The two major organs responsible for detoxing are the kidneys and liver. These two organs are very efficient in filtering out unwanted substances from our bodies. While the liver detoxifies any chemicals and medications, the kidneys filter blood and remove waste substances. The two organs pair to do a natural and perfect detoxing the body needs. So, does juices detox our bodies? The answer is no!

Taking Low-Fat Foods Helps to Lose Weight
Being in a low-fat diet does not necessarily help in weight loss. About 50,000 women went on an 8-year trial. Half of the participants went on a low-fat diet while the rest of them did not. In the end,

the women on the low-fat diet were found to have not lowered their risk to colorectal cancer, heart diseases, and breast cancer. Besides, they did not lose much weight if at all there was any.

New recommendations from different studies show that taking healthy fats in moderation is good for your health. Healthy fats include; fat from avocados, fish, and nuts. If you don't have them on your diet, add them already.

Calories Count is the Best Approach to Weight Loss
Even though watching your calories intake per day helps in losing weight, it is not the best solution when it comes to eating healthy. When used in isolation, reducing calories do not take into consideration all the required foods. The body requires proteins, carbohydrates, minerals and vitals for fuel. While counting calories is important in maintaining weight, we should not focus on it solely when improving our health.

Adding Supplements to Your Weight Loss Plan is a Good Idea
Though research has been done for decades, there is no substantial evidence of supplement's benefits. Instead, there exists evidence on the harm some of them cause. According to Harvard school professor, S Bryn Austin, the most dangerous supplements are those related to muscle building, weight loss and sexual performance.

A Diet that Works for Someone can Work for Everyone Else
Two bodies aren't the same so there can't be a single diet that can work for everyone. A healthy eating plan of an individual is influenced by different factors. The tastes and preferences, the person's schedule and their genetics. Studies

suggest that you look for a routine you can maintain. Therefore, try different plans until you find one that you like and you can stick with.

Chia seeds and Apple Cider Vinegar are Superfoods

Although there are foods that have more health benefits than others, there is no medical term or legal term as "superfoods". Health experts and nutritionists rarely use the term superfoods. Truth is, if anyone starts tossing that word around, chances are that they are just marketing the foods, or they are not as knowledgeable as they may seem.

Gluten is not Healthy for the Digestive System

Gluten does not harm you unless you suffer from celiac disease. Studies show that many people experience slight bloating and gas when they eat regardless of whether they ingest wheat or not.

Almond Milk is Healthier than Regular Milk

If you find alternatives to dairy products, they are not always nutritionally superior. For instance, a glass of low-fat milk has about 8 grams of proteins that almond milk does not have. Also, studies show that most vitamins found in almond milk are added during processing. Added vitamins reduce the body's absorption of other nutrients. However, soy milk, on the other hand, has the same amount of proteins per serving. It also has natural micronutrients derived from soybeans.

It is Better to Replace Meals with Juices

While juices might have vitamins and, in some cases, proteins, research suggests that to get these nutrients just eat a balanced diet. A diet full of fruits, vegetables, and whole-grain is the best.
Moreover, juices have less fiber in them that is essential in keeping you full. Most of the fiber is

removed while juicing. As a result, calories from sweetened juices are referred to as "empty calories". These calories will leave you hungry after some time. Besides, they affect your mood.

Microwaving Food Decreases Nutrients
A microwave uses energy waves to make the food molecules to vibrate faster in a short time. Ordinarily, some nutrients disintegrate when cooked whether by microwave, stove or oven. Since microwave cooks faster, it even keeps more nutrients intact.

CHAPTER 6

Getting Started on Healthy Eating

Margaret Mead once said that changing a man's diet is harder than changing his religion. Changing unhealthy lifestyle for the majority is a hard nut to crack. As a matter of fact, according to the 2012 study conducted in the US, 50% of the poll admitted that filing taxes are much easier than eating healthy.

From contradictory studies on food and unsustainable diets to unrealistic fitness goals; healthy eating has been a subject of controversy. It doesn't have to be that confusing. Here are the top tips on how you can start eating healthy.

Ensure you Store Healthy foods

Once you get hungry, chances are that you will go for whatever food available. Ensuring you have healthy foods available is a great way to start eating healthy. Keep healthy foods in your cupboards at home and also at your workplace. For instance, keep some fruits in a basket in your kitchen. Buy healthy snacks and store them in your pantry at eye level. In your refrigerator, stock up cooked whole grains, fruits, and vegetables. Some are of the healthy snacks to store in your office includes; dried berries, pistachios, and almonds

Avoid sugary drinks

Beverage Marketing Corporation says that an average American citizen takes about 45 gallons of soda in a year. This is a huge amount considering that these drinks have high sugar levels. Apart from the obvious diseases obesity and diabetes type 2 caused by consumption of sugar, premature aging, anxiety and liver damages are some of the many diseases. Choose to take water or unsweetened beverages if need be as opposed to drinking sweetened beverages.

Count Nutrients

Instead of focusing on calories focus on nutrients to improve the quality of your diet. Calories are different and the body can only extract energy from the quality calories.

How Do you Make Healthy Eating a Habit?

There is one simple and general rule to this. If you are unable to maintain a diet for one, two or three years, then it is not meant for you.

Many times, people tend to go on diets they cannot maintain. The main reason is that the diets are always extreme and it is hard to keep up with. As a result, they can never develop long-term healthy eating habits.

Recent statistics regarding weight loss is very frightening. Research has it that most people regain all the weight they lost just after they complete a weight loss program. Hence, always strive to balance your diet. Provided you are not on a specific dietary requirement or have a specific disease; do not eliminate certain foods off your diet.

Eliminating these foods causes cravings. At the end of the day, you may end up eating it more reducing the success of a healthy diet.

Aim to take at least 90% of whole foods while watching your potions. You will still enjoy food while you remain healthy. Besides, it is healthier than eating 90% of processed foods as many people do.

Cooking Our Way out of chronic Diseases and Obesity

Ifpress.com

Imagine going for your doctor's appointment and you are started on cooking lessons. What if the time was spent on learning culinary techniques? What if you went there to be told about grocery shopping? It is odd, but with the change in lifestyle today, it is pretty normal. There is no doubt that people who cook at home follow a healthier diet than those who don't. They are less likely to contract chronic diseases such as diabetes type 2 and obesity because they consume fewer calories.

Today scientific evidence supports teaching patients how to cook at home. It has proved to be an effective medical strategy for weight loss, improving diet and preventing diabetes. Consequently, research is focusing more on the value of nutritional programs through cooking classes. The programs have aided in eating smaller portions while adhering to a healthy diet. Such improvements were witnessed to last a year after the program ended.

Moreover, these nutritional programs have helped patients with type 2 diabetes get better by lowering blood sugars and losing weight. It is not easy to believe, but it is time to focus in the kitchen as it has proved to be a valuable medication to some of these chronic conditions.

The Solution is In the Kitchen
The biggest obstacles to eating healthy are time and money. Come to think of it, they are not true obstacles. For example, recent studies show that Americans spend an average of 2 hours a day on the internet. Remember this is something that didn't exist 20 years ago. Today, we can't find time to go grocery shopping, planning and cooking for our families. How then does it become an obstacle?
Unprocessed foods are affordable to many. Indeed, studies show that eating processed foods is more expensive than eating unprocessed foods. We have to think twice about the value we put in food. What we don't spend on eating healthy will be spent on booking doctor's appointments and treating diseases associated with being unhealthy which are many.

Flickr.com

It is time to cook our way out of bad eating habits. The decline in home cooking does not only affect our health but our families and community at large. Cooking can be fun if you put your mind to it. Besides, it is freeing and it is the only way to achieve healthiness. Home-cooked meals also aid in resilience towards anxiety, depression, and stress. In the end, we will eradicate almost all of the related diseases and become happy.

Furthermore, cooking at home does not mean you have to spend the entire day in the kitchen. It doesn't mean that you have to mix hundreds of ingredients or follow complicated recipes. Besides, the simple recipes turn out to be the tastiest. You also don't have to be a successful chef to be cooking. Use whatever experience and abilities you may have to prepare healthy meals. You will not only experience the mental benefits but also physical health benefits.

CONCLUSION

Being healthy is not just about food. Being healthy means not just physically but also mentally and emotionally. Making healthy living it a lifestyle can have long term health benefits. Taking good care of your health will not just make you feel good about yourself, but will also improve your self-image and self-esteem. This means you must keep eating healthy. Reduce carbohydrates and fats from your diet and replace them with more fruits and vegetables. You must also avoid sweets and junk at all costs.

People also think that skipping meals can help with their overall health and weight loss. Avoid skipping meals because it only ends up making the body crave for more food when you finally decide to eat.

In addition to healthy meals try to keep active as much as possible. You don't have to break your back with intense gym workouts. You can stick to a regular twenty to thirty minutes swimming, walking or floor exercises daily. Work around what your body is comfortable doing.

The more you eat healthily, the more natural it will feel to reach out for an apple or an orange instead of a piece of cake or a bag of chips when we feel hungry. Therefore, this is not a matter of starving ourselves but it is just a conscious decision of being respectful of what's best for our body in the long run. When we recognize healthy choices in our eating habits we also contribute to the general wellness of our planet. In so many ways, our personal eating choices have consequences in many ways.

Start making small changes now. Gradual changes are much easier to maintain than huge changes introduced at once. If a healthy lifestyle becomes a habit, the benefits are numerous. Remember, eating

the right foods for your health should be a lifelong
commitment. It will be important to practice self-
control to stay clear from all the fast foods and junk
foods being sold cheaply today.

With all this information the most important thing is to
stick by and maintain your decision to live healthily.
You can keep track of your choices by keeping a food
journal. You can also talk to other people when
temptations to indulge kick in. Those people can
motivate you to stick to your healthy course.

In the end, eating healthy is not about boring choices
or being unable to enjoy indulgences, it is about
gaining the right skills for a lifelong decision; a longer,
more meaningful life, improved self-esteem and self-
worth, ability to enjoy more natural tastes and the
delight of respecting our bodies for all that it.

www.ingramcontent.com/pod-product-compliance
Lightning Source LLC
Chambersburg PA
CBHW051128250726

48655CB00007B/2952